AF270981

THE SPRING ACTIVITY BOOK

Susan Vesey

Illustrated by
Simon Bull and Anna Carpenter

A LION BOOK
Tring · Batavia · Sydney

ABOUT THIS BOOK

Everyone loves springtime. The short, dark days of winter are over. The sun begins to warm the ground and all the spring flowers come into bloom. It's a time of new life in nature, when many creatures have their young. Birds get busy too, building their nests and laying their eggs.

There is celebration in the air in the springtime, too, in the days that lead up to Easter – for many people the greatest celebration of the whole year. Because Easter is not just chocolate eggs and baby chicks and Easter bunnies – fun though all these things are. Turn to the story pages in this book and you will find out why. There are lots of ideas and activities, too, to make the most of this very special time of year.

Enjoy the spring – and have a very happy Easter!

THINGS TO MAKE AND DO

Plants from pips
Sprouting beans
Springtime gift
Make a bird scarer
Rainy day game
Paper windmills
Wind chimes
Make a pancake –
    sweet or savoury
Mardi Gras mask
Decorate a simnel cake
Make crystallized flowers
Make a palm cross
Marzipan stuffed dates
Make an Easter gift
Making Easter cards
Eggshell mosaic

How to make hot cross buns
Decorating eggs
Easter baskets
Make a flapping chick
Make an Easter garden
Easter bonnet
Candle decorating

SPECIAL FEATURES

MOTHER'S DAY CARD

You can make a special card using the back cover of this book.

1. Cut just inside the dotted lines and fold the card in half.

2. Choose your own colours to complete the picture or use the printed guide to help you.

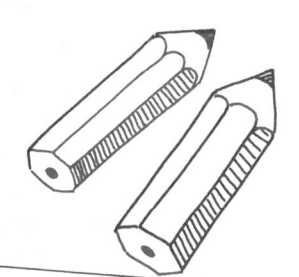

3. Write your message on the inside, and give on Mother's Day.

EASTER CARDS

1. Turn to the middle of your *Spring Activity Book* and loosen the staples.

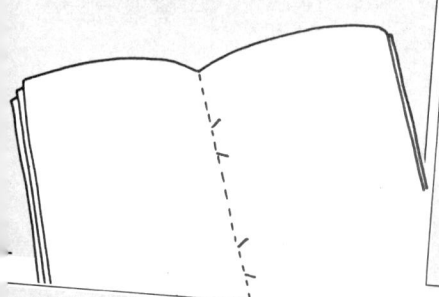

2. Pull out the card, leaving the rest of the book in one piece.

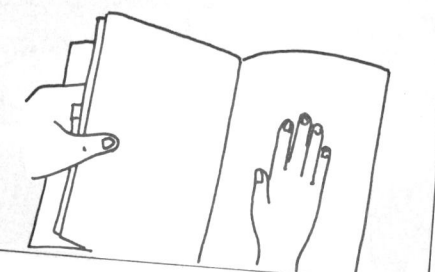

3. Cut along the dotted lines and fold each card in half.

Write your message on the inside and to someone you will not see at Easter.

NEWSPAPER FEATURE

Be a reporter and work on a special Easter edition of your own newspaper. Or use some of the ideas to produce your own Easter play, writing the scripts for each character. Turn to pages 30–31 for details.

IT'S SPRINGTIME

Seeds are sprouting, insects are hatching, and many birds and animals have their young. There is new life everywhere. You can share in it too. Try growing plants from pips or sprouting beans and you can watch the everyday miracle of new life – green shoots coming from seeds that look dead until we put them in the moist, damp earth.

PLANTS FROM PIPS

If you are not in any hurry, it is fun to see if you can grow anything from pips. Apples, oranges and grapes may all grow to give a pretty houseplant. Just poke the pips into some seed compost in a clean yoghurt pot and keep it moist and in the dark until the first sign of life appears. Then bring the pot out into the daylight, and watch the plant grow.

If you can get hold of the stone from an avocado pear, try this.

1. Poke four cocktail sticks into the stone, as shown.

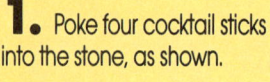

2. Dip the pointed end of the stone into the tip of a jam jar full of water. The cocktail sticks keep the stone from falling in. Keep the water level topped up.

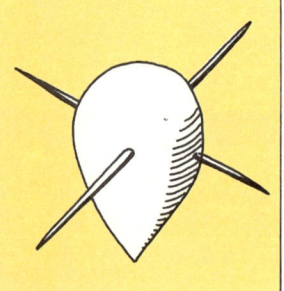

3. Several weeks (and lots of smelly water!) later a small root forces its way out of the stone and into the water. If you have any liquid plant food, add one drop at this stage. The root system continues to form and the shoot then develops.

4. When the plant has four leaves, transfer it to a flower pot and use a fine soil or compost to make sure the plant stays healthy. You can leave the cocktail sticks in or take them out very carefully.

MAKE A BIRD SCARER

Although there is plenty of natural food available for the birds in the spring, few can resist newly planted seeds or young plants!

Make this bird scarer to give to a keen gardener you know.

You will need:
- ☐ a wire coat hanger
- ☐ circles of foil or bottle tops
- ☐ garden twine, fishing line, or wool, cut into 30cm lengths
- ☐ a large darning needle

1. Thread your needle with the twine, fishing line or wool, and pass it through the top of the first circle of foil. Then take it back through the bottom of the foil.

2. Make a knot to keep the foil in place and go on to the next, so that there are 8–10 circles on each length of twine.

3. Tie the lengths of decorated twine onto the bottom of the coat hanger. Your bird scarer is ready to use! Hang it on a tree branch or on a cane stuck in the ground near the new seeds.

SPRINGTIME GIFT

If you know someone who is a keen gardener, make this useful bag for holding garden twine.

You will need:
- ☐ string
- ☐ a ball of garden twine
- ☐ sacking or plain fabric
- ☐ scissors
- ☐ paint

MATCH THEM UP!

Can you match these animals and their young? (See page 32 for answers.)

cat	fawn
dog	cub
goat	calf
cow	kitten
goose	tadpole
frog	leveret
deer	pup
sheep	foal
horse	cygnet
kangaroo	puppy
duck	piglet
hare	lamb
pig	gosling
lion	joey
seal	kid
swan	duckling

1. Cut your sacking or fabric into an oblong and fold in half to find the middle.

2. Cut a buttonhole a little higher up than the fold line, about halfway across the fabric. Neaten the edge with buttonhole stitches.

3. Cut two holes at each outer end of the fabric for the handles.

4. Paint a mouse shape and corn above the first hole with the words 'Pull my tail!'

5. Fold the fabric in half again so the mouse is on the inside. Machine-stitch the outside edges together or use small back-stitches. Leave the top open!

6. Turn the bag inside out so the mouse is on the outside again. Cut two pieces of string. Poke each piece through the holes and knot the ends to make the handles.

7. Put a ball of garden twine inside the bag with the end poking through the hole to make the tail.

SPROUTING BEANS

Alfalfa, sunflower seeds, mung beans, chick peas, aduki beans, whole lentils – all these can be sprouted very easily. They are delicious in salads or stir fried, very nutritious – and fun to grow.

You will need:
- ☐ a clean jar
- ☐ a piece of clean fabric
- ☐ an elastic band
- ☐ a tablespoon of beans

1. Soak the beans overnight in clean water.

2. Drain them and put them in the jar. Cover the jar with a piece of fabric and use the elastic band to keep it in place.

3. Keep the beans in the dark, but rinse them with clean water 3 or 4 times a day.

4. The beans will quickly sprout shoots. When these are about 5cm long, bring them into the sunlight for a few hours. They are now ready to eat.

WET & WINDY DAYS

Spring days are not always warm and sunny! Try these ideas if you have to stay inside.

RAINY DAY GAME

You will need:
- ☐ card
- ☐ plasticine
- ☐ drawing pin
- ☐ beans or counters

1. Cut a circle of card 15cm across the middle.

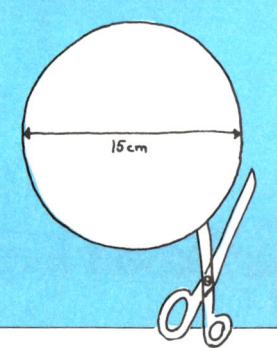

15cm

2. Cut out a pointer from the card 11cm long.

11cm

3. Divide the circle into six equal segments and write one of the instructions below in each segment.

- ○ Put one in kitty
- ○ All take one out of kitty
- ○ Take two out of kitty
- ○ All put one in kitty
- ○ Put two in kitty
- ○ Take one from each player

4. Find the centre of balance on the pointer, and push the drawing pin up through the card circle, through the pointer and into a small bead of plasticine.

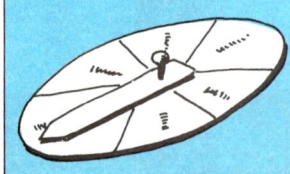

5. Give each player six beans or counters and put another six in the kitty.

6. Take it in turns to spin the pointer and follow the instruction in the segment where it lands.

Anyone who runs out of beans drops out. The winner is the person left with all the beans!

WIND CHIMES

If you collect some sea shells next time you are by the sea, you can use the bird scarer idea to make some Japanese wind chimes.

You will need lots of shells, and some help to make holes in the shells. When you have put them together, hang them up near an open window or outside, and you will hear the gentle noise they make when the wind blows.

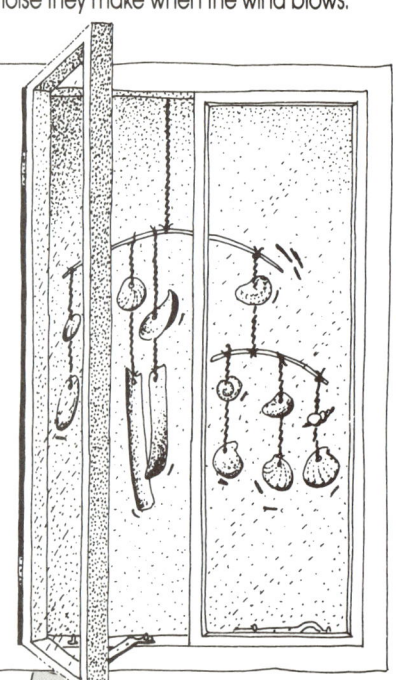

WORD GAME

Re-arrange the first letters of your answers to find the puzzle word. (Answers on page 32.)

- ☐ What eggs are doing downhill
- ☐ In the pen
- ☐ Toss this before you eat it
- ☐ A spring celebration
- ☐ Mardi ??
- ☐ Blossoms need these
- ☐ Comes before Thursday
- ☐ A feature of this book
- ☐ A special treat at tea-time
- ☐ A dozen

PAPER WINDMILLS

You can't see the wind, but with this paper windmill, you can see what it does!

You will need:
- ☐ a square of paper
- ☐ a coin
- ☐ a paper fastener
- ☐ scissors
- ☐ a needle
- ☐ 30cm long cane

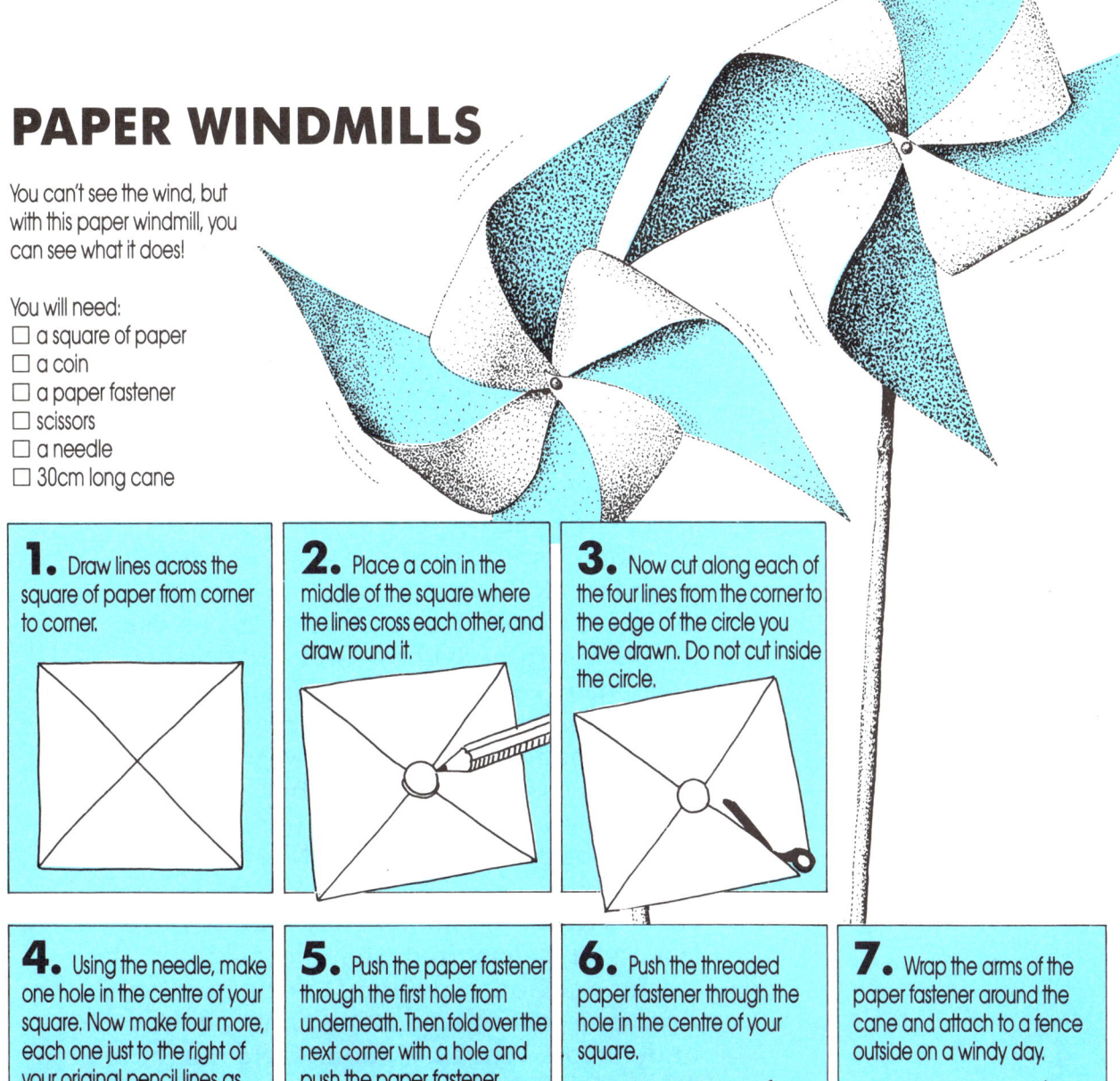

1. Draw lines across the square of paper from corner to corner.

2. Place a coin in the middle of the square where the lines cross each other, and draw round it.

3. Now cut along each of the four lines from the corner to the edge of the circle you have drawn. Do not cut inside the circle.

4. Using the needle, make one hole in the centre of your square. Now make four more, each one just to the right of your original pencil lines as shown in the diagram.

5. Push the paper fastener through the first hole from underneath. Then fold over the next corner with a hole and push the paper fastener through that. Continue until all four corners are bent over (but not creased) and threaded onto the fastener.

6. Push the threaded paper fastener through the hole in the centre of your square.

7. Wrap the arms of the paper fastener around the cane and attach to a fence outside on a windy day.

THE EASTER STORY

The best stories are the ones with a happy ending. The greatest story of all has a happy ending. The Easter story. But the story begins many years before.

You know about Jesus. He was the baby born to be king. He wasn't born in a king's palace, he was born in a stable in a backyard. This is what we remember at Christmas. Jesus was not rich like a king, with servants to help him. Instead, he grew up in an ordinary family. But Jesus was a very special baby – God's own Son – and when he grew up the things he did and said astonished people.

When Jesus was twelve years old, his parents took him to Jerusalem to celebrate the Jewish Passover. This was when the Jewish people remembered how God had rescued them many centuries before when they were slaves in Egypt. Now that their land was ruled by the Romans, many of the Jews were waiting for the 'Messiah', a king sent by God who would come and rescue them once more. On the way back from Jerusalem, Mary and Joseph realized that Jesus had got lost in the large crowds travelling home. They found him, at last, in Jerusalem, in the temple, talking to the teachers of God's laws, and asking questions. Everyone was amazed at how much he understood. When his parents told him how worried they had been, he simply replied, 'Surely you knew I had to be in my Father's house.' His parents did not understand until many years later what he really meant.

Jesus grew up and became a carpenter, working with Joseph in Nazareth. When Jesus was about thirty he began to do the work that God his Father sent him to do.

At that time a man called John (the cousin of Jesus) was attracting crowds of people out in the desert. He was preaching and teaching people about God. 'Get ready! God's King is coming!' he said. 'Change your ways, and God will forgive you.' Many of the people who heard the message wanted to live better lives, and to serve God. So John took them down to the River Jordan and 'baptized' them in the water as a sign that their sins had been washed away.

One day Jesus came to John to be baptized. At once John knew that Jesus was the King promised by God. John's first words were, 'But I'm the one who needs to be made clean, not you.' But Jesus insisted. When Jesus came up out of the water, he heard a voice saying: 'You are my own dear Son. I am pleased with you.'

Then Jesus spent forty days alone in the desert. He was very hungry and there was no food. God's enemy, Satan, began to tempt him to use his special powers in the wrong way. He wanted to make Jesus disobey God and spoil his work. It was a struggle to resist but Jesus refused to listen to Satan's suggestions. 'Go away, Satan!' he said, and God's enemy was beaten. Jesus was now ready to start the work he came to do.

Story continued on page 14

PANCAKES & PARTY TIME

Have you ever heard people say 'I'm giving it up for Lent'?

Lent is the name given to the forty days before Easter. It reminds us of the forty days Jesus spent in the desert before he began his work of teaching and healing (see story page 1).

In the Middle Ages, Lent was a time of fasting. This meant that people went without such food as meat, eggs and cream. On the day before Lent began, they used up all the fats in the house by making pancakes and enjoying the kinds of food they would go without until Easter. All sorts of games were played in the streets to celebrate before the fast began.

In some countries the day before Lent is called Mardi Gras – Fat Tuesday – and in other countries Pancake Day or Shrove Tuesday. Why Shrove Tuesday? On the day before Lent began, people went to church to ask God to forgive them for all the things they had done wrong. The word for this was 'shriving' and the word 'Shrove' comes from that.

GIVING UP AND GIVING TO . . .

Many people still give up eating something they enjoy during Lent – perhaps sweet things – and give the money they would have spent to feed the hungry of the world.

Why not ask others in your family or your class at school to do this with you? You could send the money to an organization that works in the poorer countries of the world. See page 32 for suggestions.

MAKE A PANCAKE

You will need:
- [ ] 4oz plain flour
- [ ] pinch of salt
- [ ] 1 egg
- [ ] ½ pint milk

1. Sift the flour and salt into a large bowl.

2. Break the egg into the mixture.

3. With a wooden spoon, stir the egg into the flour and salt.

4. Stir in a little milk and smooth out the lumps.

5. Gradually stir in the rest of the milk until the mixture is smooth.

6. Leave the batter in a cold place for at least 30 minutes.

Ask for help to cook the pancakes. They need a very hot frying pan and are difficult to cook properly.

Try these savoury and sweet pancakes too!

SAVOURY OR SWEET

This simple filling uses already prepared frozen foods. You could prepare it while an adult is cooking the pancakes.

You will need:
- [ ] 1 bag of frozen fish in sauce for 4 people
- [ ] 2oz frozen peas
- [ ] 2oz frozen sweetcorn

1. Cook the frozen foods following the instructions on the packets.

2. Flake the fish while it is still warm.

3. Mix the fish with the cooked vegetables.

4. When a pancake is ready, put a large spoonful of the mixture in the centre, fold over and serve.

Use any of your favourite fruits as a filling to make a delicious sweet pancake, or pour on a spoonful of golden or maple syrup.

Try one of the following:
- [ ] Stewed apples
- [ ] Strawberries
- [ ] Blueberries
- [ ] Sliced banana with lemon juice and sugar
- [ ] Gooseberries
- [ ] Blackcurrants
- [ ] Mincemeat

MARDI GRAS MASK

Mardi Gras is a time for fun and dressing up. If you can join in with the celebrations near you, make a colourful mask to add to the excitement.

You will need:
- [ ] a paper plate
- [ ] glue
- [ ] coloured pens or paint
- [ ] a doily
- [ ] feathers
- [ ] sequins
- [ ] a can of spray paint (optional)
- [ ] an old headscarf or tea towel
- [ ] some elastic

1. Draw the shape of your mask onto the paper plate. Both sides of the shape can be the same or you could make them different from each other.

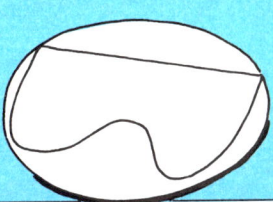

2. Cut two fairly large eyeholes, one on either side of the centre line. Cut larger holes than you think you need – you can always paint your face under the mask!

3. Make a small hole near the edge of the mask on either side and thread elastic or ribbon through each one, knotting them when the mask is complete.

4. Begin to decorate the mask with paint, feathers, beads, patterns from a doily – anything that will stick.

5. If you have spray paint you can spray the whole mask a bright colour. Be sure to do this in the open air and do not wear the mask until the paint vapour has worn off.

6. Spray the scarf or towel (or any old piece of fabric) with silver paint.

7. Ask if you can borrow some make-up to make your face look dramatic, and then put on your head covering, securing it with elastic, and your mask.

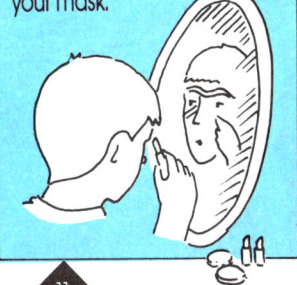

DID YOU KNOW . . . ?

The first day of Lent is called Ash Wednesday. It gets its name from a custom which began in the sixth century when Gregory was pope.

He suggested that as a sign that someone was really sorry for doing, saying or thinking something wrong, they should not wear fine clothes on that day. Instead, they should sprinkle ashes on their head and wear clothes made of sackcloth.

A DAY FOR MOTHERS

Mother's Day is a very special day for all mothers when we can thank them for all they do for us the whole year!

You could take your mother breakfast in bed or offer to do something extra to help her.

In Great Britain, the special day for mothers is celebrated on the fourth Sunday in Lent and is called Mothering Sunday. It began in the last century as the day when everyone went to the 'Mother Church' in the area instead of their local church. Children who lived and worked away from home were given the day off to visit their mothers. Sometimes they would take a cake they had baked or pick a posy of flowers on the way.

Today, some churches still celebrate Mothering Sunday by giving all mothers a small posy of flowers during the service.

The celebration of Mother's Day was started more recently in Australia, New Zealand and the USA. People often go to a special church service to thank God for their mothers. Traditionally people wore a red carnation if their mother had died and a white carnation if she was still living. Today, however, mothers tend to wear bouquets or corsages of all sorts of flowers on their clothes. Mother's Day in these countries is celebrated in May.

DECORATE A SIMNEL CAKE

There is an old tradition of giving a simnel cake to mothers as a gift on Mother's Day. It is thought that the word simnel comes from the Latin word 'simila' which means 'fine flour'.

There are a number of recipes for simnel cake today. Many of them have a layer of marzipan in the middle and are decorated in some way.

Try decorating a fruit cake with these marzipan fruits to give to your mother as a gift. Make sure your hands are very clean before you begin.

You will need:
☐ a packet of colourless marzipan
☐ edible dye in different colours

1. Break off small pieces of marzipan and shape them into different fruits.

2. Colour the different fruits as shown below.

☐ banana   yellow and brown
☐ orange   dapple the skin with the prongs of a fork
☐ peach   pink and yellow
☐ pear   green
☐ lemon   yellow

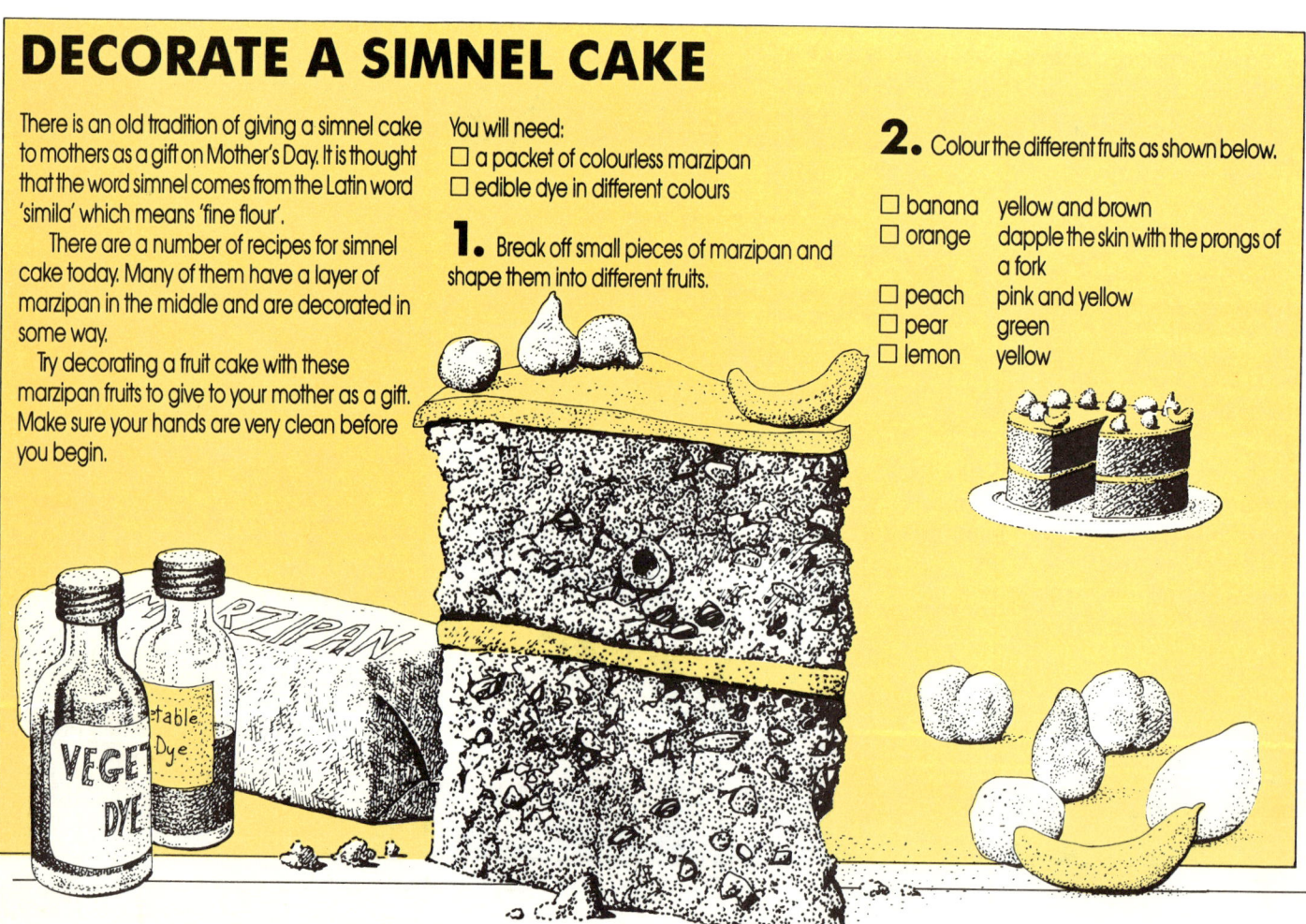

MAKE CRYSTALLIZED FLOWERS

Instead of giving your mother a posy of real flowers, why not make some crystallized flowers for her to decorate ice cream or cakes with? They take some patience to make, but the result is well worth the effort.

You will need:
- ☐ an egg white
- ☐ caster sugar
- ☐ grease-proof paper
- ☐ a new (or clean) paint-brush
- ☐ flower petals/or small flowers

1. Beat an egg white until it forms soft peaks.

2. Paint each part of the flower with the egg white until it is covered. (Do not dip it in the mixture!)

3. Using a fine sieve or a sugar dredger, pour the caster sugar over the painted flower. (Keep scooping up the extra sugar and re-using it.)

4. Put a piece of greaseproof paper on a tray or plate and lay out each flower to dry. It will take 2–3 days in a warm place such as an airing cupboard. They look lovely when finished but don't eat them.

Try these flowers:
- ☐ rose petals
- ☐ primroses
- ☐ violets
- ☐ nasturtiums
- ☐ lily of the valley
- ☐ miniature daffodils

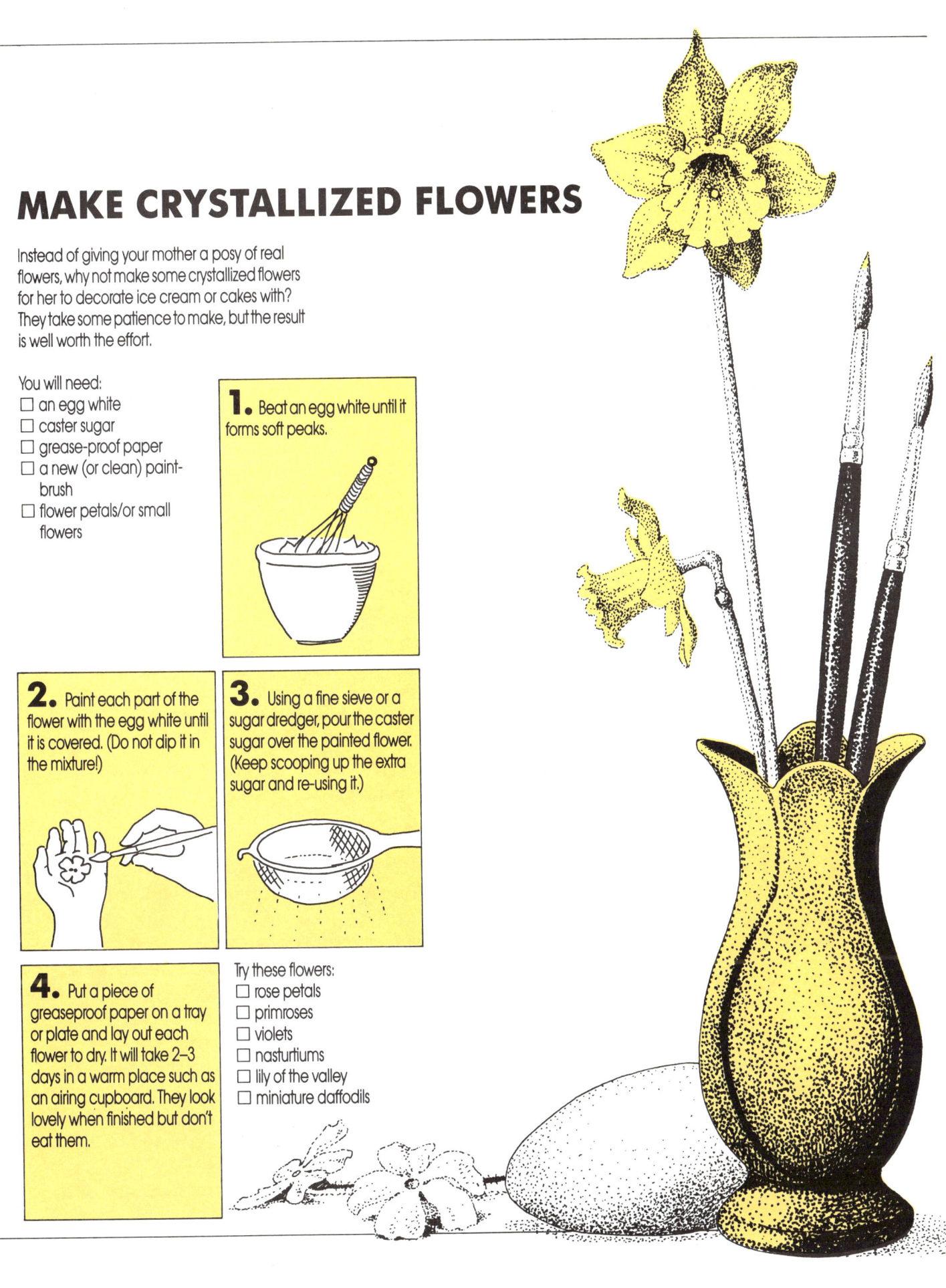

≈ PALM SUNDAY ≈

After his baptism, Jesus started to teach people about God's new Kingdom. This story is about what Jesus said and did.

Jesus returned to his home country of Galilee and began to tell the people what God had to say. 'We are living at a special time,' he said. 'The rule of God – his Kingdom – is here. You must turn away from everything that is wrong and believe God's Good News.' Before long he was followed by crowds of ordinary people, who loved to hear him talking about this new Kingdom, and to see the things he did. But in his home town of Nazareth they said, 'He's only the carpenter's son. Who does he think he is?' They tried to kill him, but he escaped.

Jesus travelled far and wide to the villages and towns around. He became very well known as someone who was always ready to help. The first miracle he did was at a wedding reception in Cana. They ran out of wine, and Jesus turned water into wine. When his friends saw this they began to believe the things he said.

Jesus cared for everyone. He was a doctor to the people who were ill. He made an old man see again and a young girl run again.

When Jesus met people who had done bad things which made them miserable and unpopular, he explained that God is a loving Father who will forgive the wrong things we think and do if we are really sorry.

He often told funny stories to make his point. 'How can you take a speck out of your friend's eye,' he said, 'if you've got a log in yours?' He wanted to remind us that we shouldn't find fault with other people without remembering our own faults!

Although Jesus had many friends and followers, he chose twelve special friends. They shared some of his closest secrets. Peter and Andrew and James and John were ordinary fishermen. They left their jobs and travelled with Jesus. The twelve special friends were with Jesus for the next three years, listening to his teaching, and seeing the miracles he did. 'You will do the same things as I do,' Jesus promised them. Years later these men travelled many miles, telling people about the Good News of God's Kingdom.

Many people believed that Jesus was special and sent by God. They turned away from doing bad things and became followers of Jesus. But some people – especially the religious leaders – did not like what Jesus did. They thought he wasn't 'religious' enough and he mixed with the wrong people. These leaders disapproved of what he did. Some of them were jealous of him. But Jesus was too clever for them. Nothing would stop him doing God his Father's work.

At the end of three years, Jesus and his disciples joined the crowds going to Jerusalem for the great Passover Festival. He sent two disciples on ahead, telling them exactly what to do. They went into a nearby village and fetched a young donkey, telling the owner that Jesus needed it. No one had ever ridden it before, but when Jesus sat on its back the donkey stood still and quiet. Jesus rode into the capital city of Jerusalem.

The news that Jesus was coming spread quickly, and crowds of people flocked to welcome him. They crowded the narrow streets and cheered as Jesus rode by. They were so thrilled and excited to see him. Some of the crowd threw their cloaks onto the road to carpet his way. Others broke off branches from palm trees and waved them like flags. Everyone shouted for joy. This was Jesus, the healer, the man of God, who had done wonderful miracles. They welcomed him like a king. 'Here comes God's King!' they shouted. 'Praise God!'

Story continued on page 20

15

PALMS & CROSSES

The Sunday before Easter Day is the first day of Holy Week, the week leading up to Easter. It is known as Palm Sunday, because when Jesus rode into Jerusalem, the people spread palm branches on the road in front of him.

Many churches today give out crosses made of palm leaves to remind people of the event.

MARZIPAN STUFFED DATES

Make this tasty gift to give as an Easter present.

You will need:
- ☐ 8oz dessert dates
- ☐ ¼lb marzipan
- ☐ caster sugar
- ☐ 1oz chocolate

1. Slit the date neatly and carefully remove the stone.

2. Roll small pieces of marzipan into shapes like the stone you have just taken out.

3. Coat each marzipan shape in sugar and slip it inside a date.

4. Break the squares of chocolate into a cup.

5. Put some hand-hot water into a bowl.

6. Put the cup of broken chocolate into the bowl of water. This will melt the chocolate, but be careful not to let any water splash into the cup or the chocolate will go cloudy.

7. Use a teaspoon to pour a little melted chocolate over each marzipan date.

8. Leave to set.

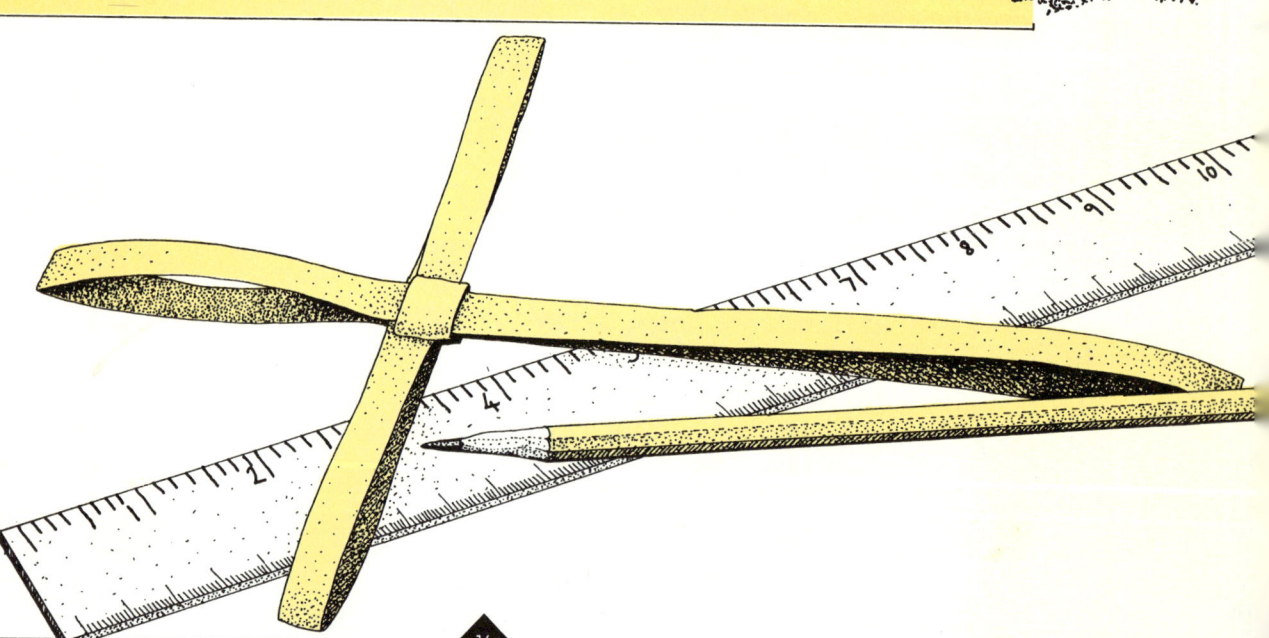

MAKE A PALM CROSS

A real palm cross is made of palm leaf. This method uses thin card which may be easier to find!

You will need:
- [ ] 1 strip of thin card 1cm wide and 27cm long
- [ ] 1 strip of thin card 1cm wide and 35cm long
- [ ] ruler
- [ ] pencil

1. Using the shorter strip of card, make a mark at the 1cm, 2cm, 3cm, 9cm and 21cm points.

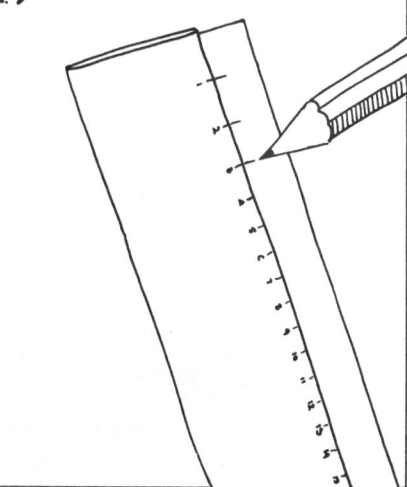

2. Fold the card neatly at each point as shown in the diagram.

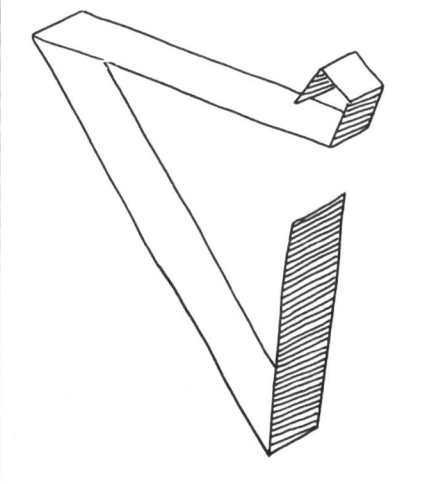

3. Flatten the card to make the cross-beam but make sure there is a gap through the middle of the little folds. Take the second strip of card and tuck one end into this gap. Don't let it come right through the other side.

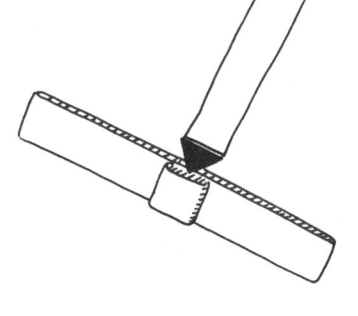

4. Take the other end of the long strip and loop it over the cross-beam. Push the end through the gap behind the first end and pull tightly.

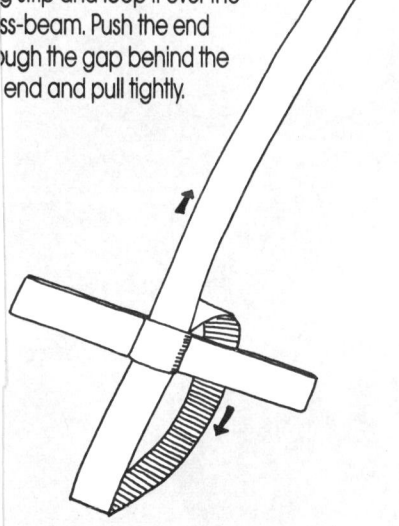

5. Measure about 6cm along the long strip from the gap and make a fold.

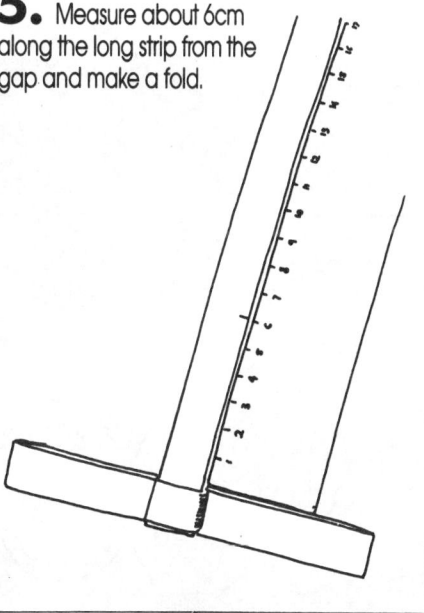

6. Push the long end back through the gap leaving the card up to the fold above the cross-beam. Your cross is now complete.

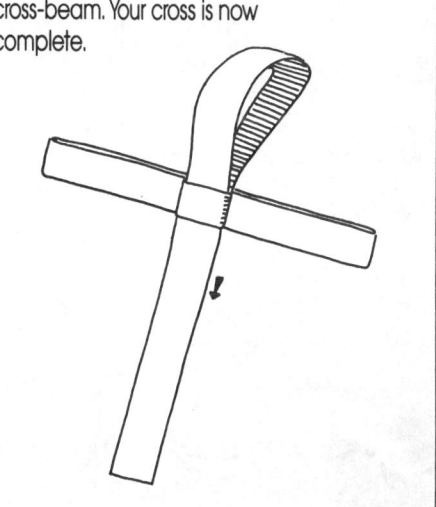

GETTING READY FOR EASTER

MAKING EASTER CARDS

Here is an idea for an Easter card which is great fun to make.

You will need:
- ☐ card
- ☐ scissors
- ☐ pinking shears
- ☐ cotton wool
- ☐ paint
- ☐ brushes
- ☐ glue
- ☐ a large wooden spoon

1. Fold the card in half.

2. Place the wooden spoon on the card with the edge of the spoon on the folded edge of the card.

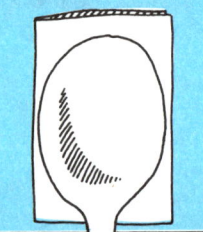

3. Draw around the spoon part. This will help you to draw a good oval.

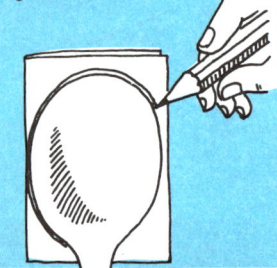

4. Cut around the edge of the oval, making sure that you do not cut away the folded edge. You need this for the hinge.

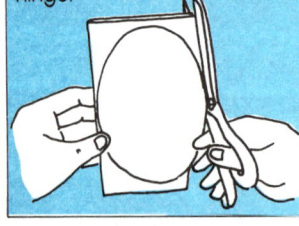

5. Open out the card.

6. Using the pinking shears, cut a zigzag line across the centre of the front as far as the hinge.

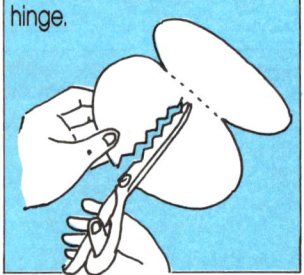

7. On the inside of the card draw a chick.

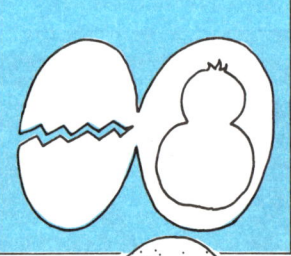

8. Tease out some yellow cotton wool and glue it over the chick.

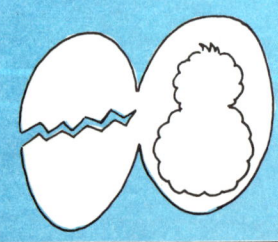

9. Draw a beak and eyes in the right places.

10. Write an Easter greeting or message inside.

A MEAL TO REMEMBER

Before Jesus and his twelve disciples had their last meal together (see story page 3) Jesus washed his disciples' feet. He was showing them that they must serve one another, if they really meant to follow his example.

Maundy Thursday has traditionally been the day when priests, monks and kings have literally followed the example set by Jesus.

Every year on this day the Pope takes part in a special service, washing the feet of twelve disabled children.

In Britain, the Queen gives out two small leather purses, one containing specially minted money, a coin for each year of her age, to twelve elderly people.

MAKE AN EASTER GIFT

The daffodil is also called the 'Lent lily' because it usually flowers in the weeks leading up to Easter. Why not make a bunch of daffodils to give to your mother on Easter Day?

You will need:
- ☐ yellow card
- ☐ tracing or grease-proof paper
- ☐ egg cartons
- ☐ orange paint
- ☐ paintbrush
- ☐ green card
- ☐ scissors
- ☐ paper fasteners
- ☐ glue or stapler

1. Trace the petal shape onto the yellow card.

2. C...ound the petals.

3. Cut the egg carton into individual pieces.

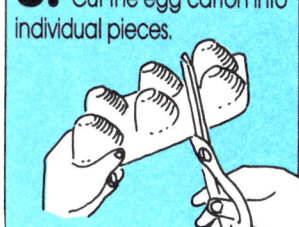

4. Paint them orange and leave them to dry.

5. Cut ... strips of green card for the ...ks.
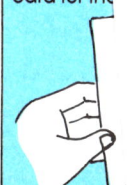

6. Cut out the leaves from the green card.

7. Put the daffodils together by pushing the paper fastener carefully through the top of the stem, then through the centre of the petal circle, and then through the base of the egg carton.

8. Open ...e fastener inside the ora...egg carton.
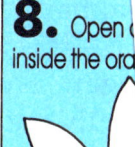
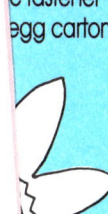

9. Glue or staple leaf to the stalk.

EGGSHELL MOSAIC

Try this idea to make a very special present for Easter. It takes lots of patience, but the results can be worth it.

You will need:
- ☐ eggshells, washed and dried
- ☐ tweezers
- ☐ glue
- ☐ card
- ☐ watercolour pens or coloured pencils

1. Draw a picture onto the piece of card.

2. Cover one area of your drawing lightly with glue.

3. Break the eggshells into small pieces and use the tweezers to pick up each piece and place it on the area you have just glued.

4. Glue and ... up the mosaic in each ... of your drawing in turn so ... the glue does not dry bef... ou have put the pieces of s... in place.

5. When the w... drawing has tiny p...s of eggshell over it, c... each part of the drawing ... complete the effec...

JESUS IS BETRAYED

Jesus' ride into Jerusalem on Palm Sunday was the beginning of the most important week in history.

Trouble had been brewing for Jesus for some time. The religious leaders and important businessmen of the city were jealous and afraid of Jesus. They had tried in the past to catch him out with clever arguments, but Jesus was always one jump ahead of them and anyway the ordinary people loved to listen to his teaching. Jesus was their hero, and the leaders were afraid of his power. So they plotted to get rid of him. But how were they to do it? They needed a spy, one of his friends who was prepared to betray him. Then Judas, one of the twelve special friends, offered to help them arrest Jesus. The chief priests were delighted. They even agreed to pay him a reward. Judas went back to the other disciples as if nothing had happened.

A few days later, the Passover celebrations began. The evening before Passover, every family had a special meal. Jesus made careful arrangements to share this meal with his disciples. Peter and John were sent ahead to a large upstairs room and got everything ready. It should have been a happy time, but when Jesus sat down to the table with the group of twelve friends they all felt sad. Jesus knew this was the last meal they would share together.

They were shocked when Jesus told them that one of them was a traitor. But Judas had made up his mind – he got up and went out into the dark night. Jesus did not stop him. When he had gone, Jesus blessed and broke a loaf of bread. He gave it to his disciples, telling them that his body would be broken like the loaf. Then he said the blessing over a cup of wine, and passed it round among the disciples saying that his blood would soon be poured out like the wine. He was about to die, for their sake.

Then he told them many things which the disciples could not understand at the time. He tried to explain about his death, and tell them that he would come alive again, but they could not accept it. Suddenly Peter burst out that he would die rather than let this happen to Jesus. But Jesus shook his head sadly. He told Peter that before daybreak he would be so afraid that he would pretend he had never even known him.

Later that evening, in the Garden of Gethsemane, Jesus began to pray, falling face down on the ground, crying out to God. The disciples, waiting nearby, fell asleep, worn out with sadness and fear. Jesus was alone. Suddenly the garden was filled with noise. Crashing through the dark trees came soldiers armed with clubs and swords. They were led by Judas who stepped forward and kissed Jesus in greeting. At this agreed sign the soldiers grabbed Jesus. Immediately Peter drew his sword and slashed out in fury. He cut off the right ear of the nearest man. But Jesus did not want violence, so he healed the man's ear and went quickly with the soldiers to the house of the high priest where the Jewish Supreme Court was waiting to try him. They fixed the evidence against him so that he would be sentenced to death.

In the courtyard outside, in a crowd of people, Peter waited anxiously for news of Jesus. As he warmed himself by the fire, a servant girl asked him whether he was one of Jesus' disciples. He was so afraid of what might happen to him that he said, 'Certainly not.' Later he was asked again, and again Peter said no. Finally someone said he was sure that he had seen Peter in the garden with Jesus, but again Peter denied it. At that moment the cock crowed, at the first light of day. In despair Peter remembered: this was just what Jesus said would happen.

Story continued on page 26

HOT CROSS BUNS

On Good Friday Christians remember Jesus' death on the cross. Even the special spicy buns we eat are marked with a cross.

HOW TO MAKE HOT CROSS BUNS

You will need:
- ☐ 8oz plain flour
- ☐ 2oz butter
- ☐ 1oz sugar
- ☐ 1 mug milk
- ☐ ¼oz dried yeast
- ☐ 1 small egg, beaten
- ☐ pinch of salt
- ☐ pinch mixed spice
- ☐ 3oz currants
- ☐ 1oz mixed peel

1. Sift the flour, salt and mixed spice into a mixing bowl.

2. Dissolve 2oz butter and 1oz sugar in a mug of just-warm milk, and add ¼oz dried yeast. Leave this for 3 minutes, stir once, and then mix in a small beaten egg.

3. Pour the liquid into the flour and beat until smooth.

4. Turn the dough onto a floured board and add the currants and mixed peel.

CROSSES

Many people wear a cross as a piece of jewellery. Because the cross means so much to Christians it has also been used in art and architecture all over the world. Look out for the following and try to find out something about them. Colour these in.

The Celtic Cross

The Maltese Cross

5. Place the dough in a well-greased polythene bag (put a spoonful of oil inside the bag and screw it up to grease it thoroughly). Put it in a warm place to make it rise.

6. When the dough has doubled in size, take it out of the bag and thump all the air out until the dough is more or less back to its original size. Cover the dough with the greased bag again, and leave it for half an hour in a warm place. The dough should rise again.

7. Shape the dough into four small round buns and mark a cross on the top of each one, using the back of a knife, a strip of pastry or a thick paste made from flour and water. To make the tops of the buns shiny, brush them with a solution of sugar and milk.

8. Leave the buns on a greased baking sheet for about 20 minutes to rise again. Bake in a hot oven (425°F or Mark 7) for 15–20 minutes. (Buns bake best in a steamy oven, so put a roasting tin full of water on the bottom of the oven to create steam.)

Always ask for help to put the buns into the oven and take them out.

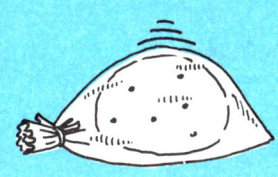

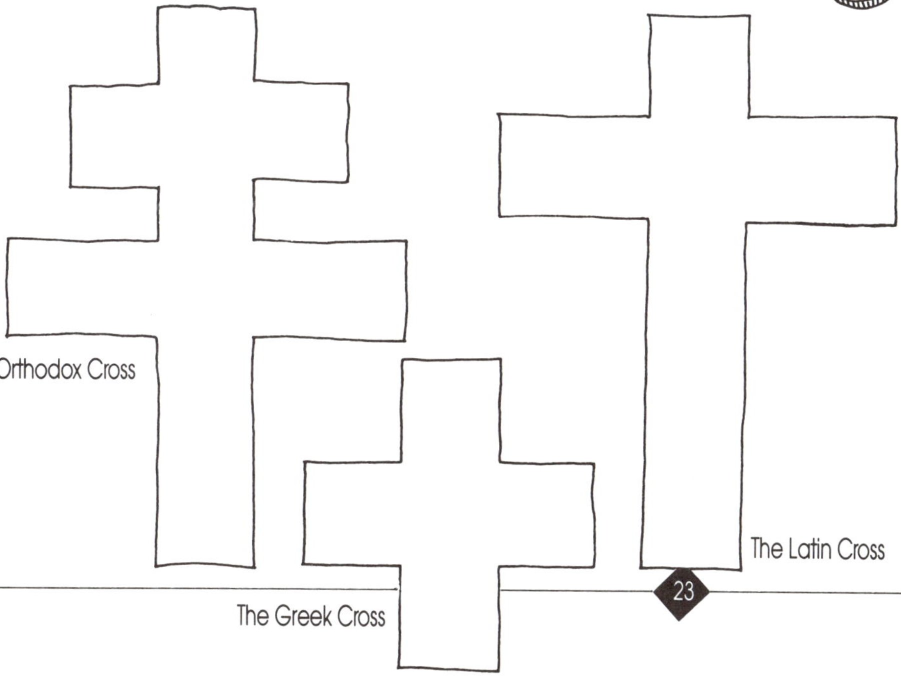

e Orthodox Cross

The Greek Cross

The Latin Cross

DID YOU KNOW?

Good Friday seems to have been called God's Friday, originally. In Germany it is called Silent Friday, and in Greece, Holy or Great Friday. But why call it 'good' when it's the day when Jesus died? His death brings forgiveness and new life for each of us: that is good news!

EGGS,EGGS,EGGS!

Why do you think eggs and Easter go together? When you've enjoyed all the eggy things to do on this page, read story page 4 and see if you can think of a reason.

DECORATING EGGS

Traditionally, hard-boiled eggs were decorated to be given to children on Easter morning. A really hard-boiled egg will last for a long time. Why not decorate some eggs this year?

METHOD 1

You will need:
- □ some eggs
- □ vegetable dye

1. Hard boil the eggs, placing a few drops of vegetable dye in the water.

2. Leave to cool.

3. Scratch off the dye to leave a white pattern underneath.

METHOD 2

You will need:
- □ some eggs
- □ onion skins
- □ spinach leaves or anemone petals or birch bark or red primula flowers
- □ pieces of material
- □ string or cotton

1. Wrap the hard-boiled egg in the onion skins or some of the leaves. You can either use a different leaf for each egg, giving eggs of a single colour; or you can use two or three different leaves on each egg, giving multi-coloured eggs.

2. Tie each egg in a piece of material and secure with string, cotton or rubber bands.

3. Hard boil the eggs in a saucepan of water.

4. Be sure the eggs are cold before you remove the bandage of material and leaves.

VEGETABLE DYES

Different leaves give different colours.
- □ Onions give yellow dye.
- □ Spinach leaves give green dye.
- □ Anemone petals give green dye.
- □ Birch bark gives purple and grey dye.
- □ Red primula flowers give blue and green dye.

EASTER BASKETS

Make some miniature baskets to hold your decorated eggs. Each basket will hold one egg. It makes a charming gift.

You will need:
- □ some coloured card or heavy paper
- □ glue or stapler
- □ tissue paper

1. Draw round a cup or small saucer placed on the card, and cut out a circle about 9cm across.

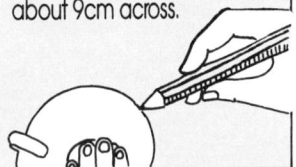

2. Cut a strip of card about 1cm wide and about 7cm long.

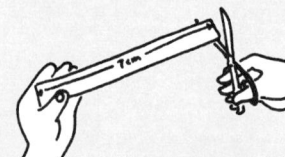

3. Curve opposite sides of the card circle upwards and glue or staple each end of the card strip to the edges of the circle. This should make a basket shape.

4. Scrunch up some tissue paper and glue it to the bottom of the basket, making an egg-shaped nest in the middle.

5. Nestle one of your decorated eggs into the tissue paper to stop it sliding out.

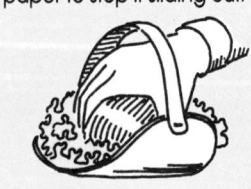

MAKE A FLAPPING CHICK

You will need:
- ☐ card
- ☐ paper fasteners
- ☐ wool
- ☐ hole puncher
- ☐ sticky tape

1. Trace or copy the shapes onto the card and cut them out.

2. Punch holes in the card where shown.

3. Thread wool through the wing holes as shown and leave the ends hanging down.

4. Using the paper fasteners, fasten the wings onto the body.

5. Cut out a lever from the card and put it through the slit from front to back.

6. Tape the wool onto the top of the lever so that the wings will flutter up and down when the lever is pulled.

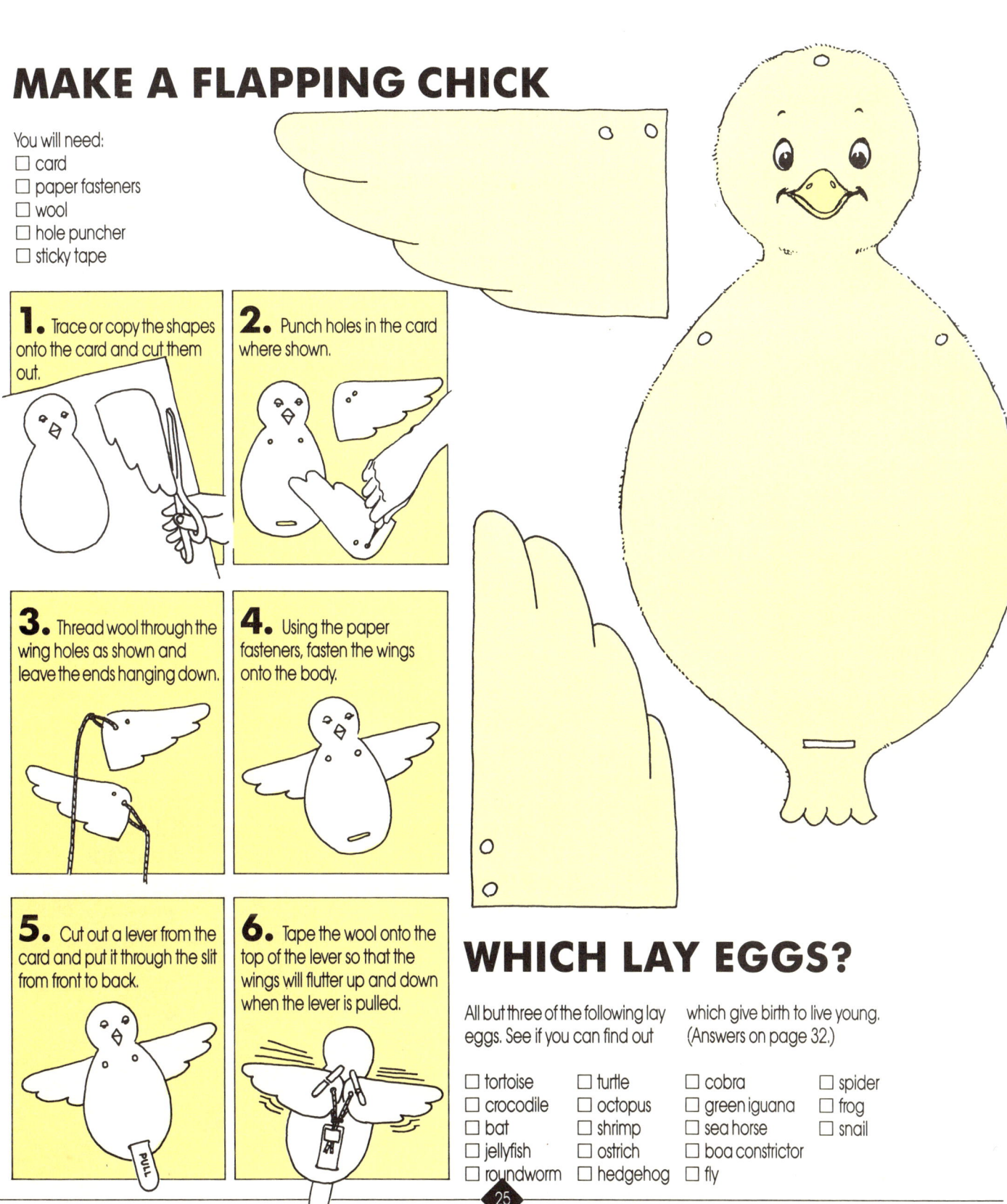

WHICH LAY EGGS?

All but three of the following lay eggs. See if you can find out which give birth to live young. (Answers on page 32.)

- ☐ tortoise
- ☐ crocodile
- ☐ bat
- ☐ jellyfish
- ☐ roundworm
- ☐ turtle
- ☐ octopus
- ☐ shrimp
- ☐ ostrich
- ☐ hedgehog
- ☐ cobra
- ☐ green iguana
- ☐ sea horse
- ☐ boa constrictor
- ☐ fly
- ☐ spider
- ☐ frog
- ☐ snail

❦ THE FIRST EASTER ❦

To Peter and the other friends of Jesus, it looked
as though all their hopes were dashed. Jesus
was taken away to be killed. How could this
story have a happy ending?

On Friday morning the Jewish court took Jesus
to the Roman governor for him to agree the
death sentence. But Pilate, the governor, did
not find Jesus guilty by Roman law. Instead he
offered to release Jesus. But the crowd cried out
for a robber named Barabbas to be released.
They wanted Jesus to be crucified. Pilate, afraid
of having a riot on his hands, gave in.

So Jesus was crucified with two criminals at
Golgotha, the Place of the Skull. Nailed to the
cross above his head was a statement of his
'crime'. It read: THIS IS JESUS OF
NAZARETH, KING OF THE JEWS. Although
Jesus was in great pain, he did not hate the men
who had put him to death. 'Father, forgive
them,' he prayed. 'They don't know what they
are doing.'

In the middle of the day a great darkness
covered the whole country for three hours, and
at the moment Jesus died an earthquake shook
the land. A soldier, watching, said, 'Surely this
was the Son of God.'

On Friday afternoon a good man called
Joseph of Arimathea was given permission to
bury Jesus decently in a tomb in a garden. Then
a huge stone was rolled in front of the entrance
and the grave was sealed.

The next day, Saturday, was the Jewish
sabbath, when the Jews were not allowed to do
any work. So at the first opportunity, very early
on Sunday morning, two women called Mary
went to the tomb. It was quiet and peaceful in
the garden after the terrible events of the past
few days. There were signs of new life all
around, hopeful comforting signs. New
flowers were opening and young birds sang in

the fresh light of sunrise. It felt like a dream to the tired women. Indeed they thought it must be a dream when they discovered that the great stone guarding the entrance of the tomb had been rolled to one side. The tomb itself was empty. The body of Jesus had gone. Confused and bewildered, the women looked inside and saw an angel there in dazzling brilliant white. 'Why are you looking in a grave for someone who is alive?' he asked. 'Remember that Jesus said he would rise from the dead. He is not here. He is alive again. Go and tell the disciples.' The disciples themselves could hardly believe such amazing news. But it was no dream. Jesus appeared before them all, first to Mary Magdalene in the garden, then later to the others.

In the days that followed, a great many of his followers saw him and spoke to him on different occasions, before he finally left them and returned to his Father in heaven. He explained how the Scriptures had foretold that he must die to suffer the punishment due to us for all our wrongdoing. When Jesus rose from the dead it proved without a shadow of doubt that Jesus really was the Son of God, as he had claimed. His followers knew now that he would do all he had promised. They were so happy and everywhere they went they told people the Good News of God's Kingdom.

So the Easter story has a happy ending. Jesus was killed but he came alive again. And he didn't leave his followers feeling lost and lonely. He sent his Spirit to be a loving comfort and strength to them. They believed in him and he gave them new life. The same Spirit of Jesus can fill us with new life, with love and strength today. That is why the Easter story never grows old.

CELEBRATING EASTER

Easter is a time of new beginnings – a time of joyful celebration! For Christians it is not just a day for chocolate eggs but one of special church services, sometimes at dawn! They celebrate the day when Jesus triumphed over death, bringing new life here and now to all who follow him, and the certainty of life after death.

MAKE AN EASTER GARDEN

Some people like to make an Easter Garden to remind them of what happened on Easter Day. If you use seeds, you need to plan a long time ahead, using the instructions on the seed packets. But if you have flowers in your garden, try this idea.

You will need:
☐ a large tin-foil dish or baking tray
☐ damp sand or peat
☐ a toilet-roll middle
☐ a large round stone

1. Fill your tray with sand or peat. Lay the toilet-roll middle on the surface, and cover with more peat to make a hill. Leave one end uncovered.

2. Place the round stone to one side of the hole to represent the stone rolled away from the empty tomb.

3. Ask if you can take some tiny bulbs from the garden (crocus or snowdrop or similar) and plant them in the peat. Use stones and leafy twigs to complete your Easter Garden.

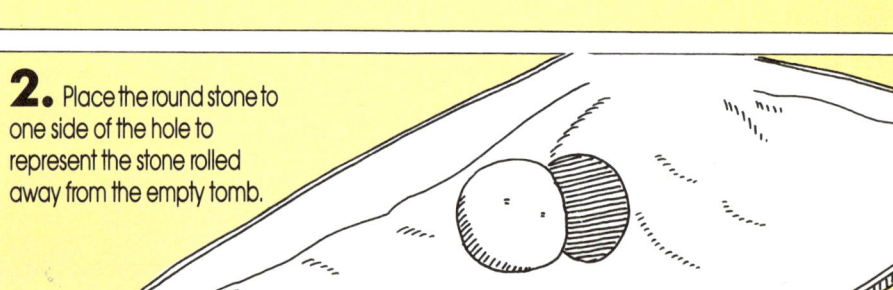
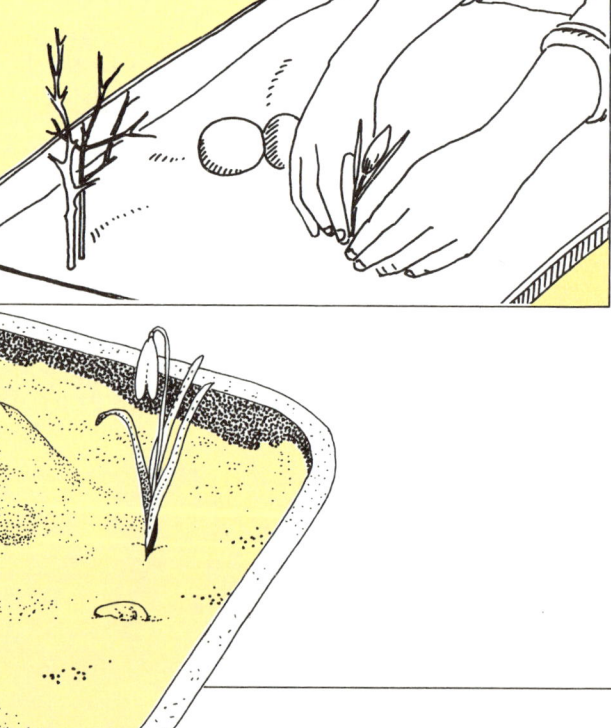

EASTER BONNET

Easter Sunday was traditionally the day when a new bonnet was worn for the first time. Make this bonnet for yourself or a sister to wear.

You will need:
- [ ] a large paper plate
- [ ] ribbon or strip of crepe paper
- [ ] large doily
- [ ] coloured tissue paper
- [ ] scissors
- [ ] thread

1. Glue the doily onto the top of the paper plate.

2. Make a narrow slit in each side of the paper plate and doily.

3. Thread through each slit enough ribbon or crepe paper to make the bonnet tie up under your chin.

Now make the paper roses to decorate the hat.

4. Fold the tissue in half lengthways. Cut the long edges into a zigzag pattern.

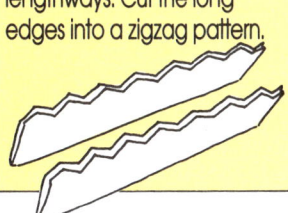

5. Concertina-fold the tissue, bunch at the middle and tie very tightly with thread.

6. Fold in half at the thread and tease out the layers of tissue all round to make a rose.

7. Glue or staple the roses onto the paper plate to complete your bonnet. Curve it round your head and tie the ribbons under your chin in a big bow.

CANDLE DECORATING

Light is an important symbol in many world religions. For Christians, Easter is the time when light finally overcame darkness, when good won the battle against evil.

You will need:
- [ ] a white wax candle
- [ ] glue
- [ ] pressed leaves and flowers
- [ ] glitter
- [ ] paintbrush
- [ ] sticky tape

1. Dip the bottom 5cm of the candle into the glue and carefully arrange the pressed leaves and flowers onto the glued area. A paintbrush will help you slide the flowers into place without breaking them.

2. Sprinkle the glitter on.

3. When the glue is dry, use a piece of sticky tape to keep the flowers secure.

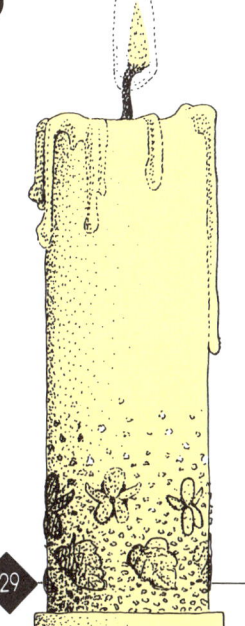

DID YOU KNOW?

Why do we call the festival Easter? Long ago the goddess Eostre (or Eastre) was worshipped with the arrival of spring. When people became Christians they kept the same name for the festival celebrating the resurrection of Jesus.

NEWSPAPER FEATURE

Why not put together a special Easter issue of your own newspaper? It would make a good project for your class at school. Or you could invite a group of friends to work on it in the Easter holidays.

HOW TO MAKE THE NEWSPAPER

1. When you have decided on the size, take one sheet of paper and fold it in half. This gives you 4 pages.

2. Fold more sheets of paper in the same way until you have the number of pages you want. Put the second folded sheet inside the first and so on.

3. Allow an area at the top of page 1 for the name of your newspaper and draw a pencil line across. Divide the rest of the sheet into columns.

4. Draw columns on the other pages in pencil. If you want a picture to go across a column you can always erase some of the lines.

SIZE AND EXTENT

You will need to decide:
- ☐ what it will be called
- ☐ what size it will be
- ☐ how many pages it will have
- ☐ how many columns per page
- ☐ whether it will be black and white or colour
- ☐ what size heading to give to each article, depending on importance

HEADINGS

If an article is very important, or 'headline news' you might show this by putting the title in capital letters or by making the letters bigger or bolder than usual – or both. For example:

MAN RISES FROM THE GRAVE

UNUSUAL HAPPENINGS IN PRIVATE GA

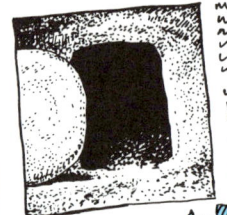

Other titles might then have capital and smaller letters or be in a smaller size. For example:

Weather Bulletin: Friday Afternoon Blackout

STAFF

If you are making your newspaper with friends, find out what people are best at and divide the work something like this.

☐ Reporters could interview people and write the articles in notebooks
☐ Researchers could check the facts
☐ Editors could check the spelling and make sure the articles fit the space

☐ Printers could write out the edited articles onto the newspaper in their neatest writing
☐ Photographers could find pictures to support the articles (or draw them!) and stick them in

Remember to put the name of each person under their work. For example:

John James, reporting from Jerusalem
or Picture by Katie Walker

CONTENT

Here are some ideas for articles based on the events of the Easter story and other items in this book. Imagine that you are in Jerusalem nearly 2,000 years ago . . .

HEADLINE NEWS

'DEAD MAN SEEN ALIVE'

Write a brief report on the events leading up to the resurrection of Jesus, ending with the startling news of Jesus being seen alive.

SUPPORTING PICTURE

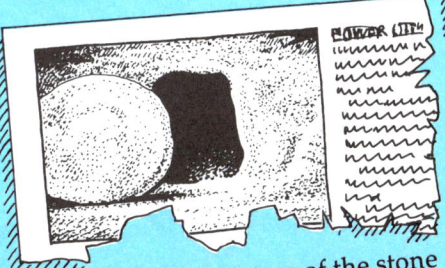

Draw your own picture of the stone rolled away from the tomb.

OTHER NEWS REPORTS

Interview people who see the story from different points of view, or who have interesting stories to tell.

'WOMAN SPEAKS TO MAN WHO DIED'

An interview with Mary in the garden.

'FRIEND WHO RAN AWAY'

An interview with Peter about the night before Jesus' death and what has happened since.

'CHANGED LIFE OF MAN IN THE TREE'

An interview with Zacchaeus.

'THE KING ON A DONKEY – EYE-WITNESS REPORT'

Talk to someone in the crowd about Jesus' entry into Jerusalem.

'BLIND MAN SEES!'

An interview with someone who has been healed by Jesus.

Your researchers will need to check the facts! Use a modern translation of a Bible, if you can, and turn to the New Testament section. The first four books are called Gospels – which means 'good news' – and contain lots of stories about Jesus. These references will help you find the ones you need.

☐ John's Gospel, chapter 20:10–18
☐ Matthew's Gospel, chapter 26:17–30
☐ Luke's Gospel, chapter 19:1–10
☐ John's Gospel, chapter 12:12–19
☐ Mark's Gospel, chapter 10:46–52

QUIZ OR CROSSWORD

Make up your own questions and answers.

ANSWERS

MATCH THEM UP!
(page 5)

cat	kitten
dog	puppy
goat	kid
cow	calf
goose	gosling
frog	tadpole
deer	fawn
sheep	lamb
horse	foal
kangaroo	joey
duck	duckling
hare	leveret
pig	piglet
lion	cub
seal	pup
swan	cygnet

WORD GAME
(page 6)

Rolling
Ink
Pancake
Easter
Gras
Insects
Maundy
Newspaper
Simnel cake
Twelve

SPRINGTIME

GIVING UP AND GIVING TO . . .
(page 10)

Save The Children Fund
Mary Datchelor House
17 Grove Lane
London
SE5

OXFAM
274 Banbury Road
Oxford
OX2 7DZ

Christian Aid
240 Ferndale Road
London
SW9 8BH

Tear Fund
100 Church Road
Teddington
Middx
TW11 8QE

WHICH LAY EGGS?
(page 25)

bat
hedgehog
boa constrictor

Copyright © 1987 Lion Publishing

Published by
Lion Publishing plc
Icknield Way, Tring, Herts, England
ISBN 0 7459 1015 7
Lion Publishing Corporation
1705 Hubbard Avenue, Batavia, Illinois 60510, USA
ISBN 0 7459 1015 7
Albatross Books Pty Ltd
PO Box 320, Sutherland, NSW 2232, Australia
ISBN 0 86760 868 4

First edition 1987
Reprinted 1988

Graphics by Tony Cantale Graphics

Printed and bound in Belgium